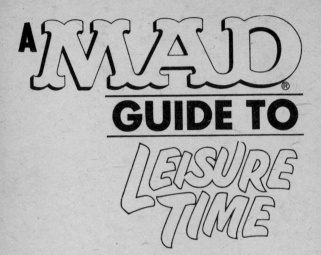

A MAD GUIDE TO LEISURE TIME

WRITTEN BY DICK DE BARTOLO

ILLUSTRATED BY GEORGE WOODBRIDGE

EDITED BY NICK MEGLIN

WARNER BOOKS

A Warner Communications Company

CONTENTS

Chapter I
CAMPING   Page 5

Chapter II
SAILING   Page 25

Chapter III
GARDENING   Page 45

Chapter IV
CYCLING   Page 61

Chapter V
DRAWING AND PAINTING   Page 77

Chapter VI
GOLF   Page 93

Chapter VII
SNORKELING   Page 105

Chapter VIII
DO-IT-YOURSELF   Page 125

Chapter IX
BOWLING   Page 141

Chapter X
WEIGHTLIFTING   Page 143

Chapter XI
HUNTING   Page 155

Chapter XII
FLYING   Page 173

We would like to thank the following experts for making this book useful and informative as it is:

CAMPING—Bill La Cour

SAILING—Nordskog, Brown, Whorrall, Flint & Co.

GARDENING—Norman Blagman

CYCLING—Bill Negron

DRAWING & PAINTING—Murray Tinkelman

GOLF—Howard Todman

SNORKELING—Ed Bacon

DO-IT-YOURSELF—Guy Barbaro

BOWLING—Andy Nickerson

WEIGHTLIFTING—Tom Ireland

HUNTING— Oscar Hyman

FLYING— Jack Drury

CHAPTER I

CAMPING

Perhaps the easiest and one of the least expensive leisure time activities is *camping*. The latest Department of Interior report states that last year some 60 million people went on overnight camping trips. Unfortunately, 58 of that 60 million went out on the same weekend which did cut down somewhat on the feeling of being alone in the wilderness.

Yes, overnight camping does lead one to a spirit of adventure, to a self-satisfaction that he can survive on his own, and, perhaps most important of all, a chance to be away from the hustle and bustle of everyday living. But although a scene like the one below depicting a minimal camp set-up appears to be free of problems...

...problems do exist! Like getting up every hour all night long to put coins in the parking meter, getting hit with garbage from neighbor's windows, being mugged, etc. For these reasons the serious camper is advised to seek more suitable environs, such as a backyard in the suburbs!

HIKING

Your legs are all the transportation you need to be a camper. Exotic campsites are closer than you think—out of the cab, across the patio, through the entrance, up to the ticket counter, through the waiting room, up the steps, and there you are—on a plane to a wonderful vacationland where you don't have to walk a step!

BACKPACKING

All your gear is carried in a pack. Lightweight frames enable you to keep the load down to under 35 pounds which becomes even less as the trip progresses and food and supplies are used up...

START OF TRIP   **MIDDLE OF TRIP**

END OF TRIP

YOUR FEET

The most important gear you will invest in will be your hiking boots. This is not the place to save money. A good pair of hiking boots are your key to having a good trip, so rather than spend $15 on a pair of cheap boots, wait until you have double that sum before you go shopping. If you can't wait and don't have the $30 necessary, see if you can convince one of your buddies to become a partner on a good pair of hiking boots...

Remember, your feet are your best friends on a trip, so treat them well. Besides washing them often and the usual massages, why not take them to dinner once in awhile, and perhaps a movie afterwards. They deserve it!

BUILDING-UP

Practice makes perfect, even in hiking. One experienced hiker used his apartment building to train his legs and body for an upcoming trip. Every day he would put on his full field pack and walk up the eight stories, once the first day, twice the second, and so on until he could do it 8 times without becoming over-exhausted. At this point he climbed to the 77th floor of a huge office building and camped there for a week...

PACKING

Packing is an *art* and also takes lots of practice before it can be mastered. Tents, stoves, sleeping bags, cooking gear, and other gear usually come in neat, compact containers from the manufacturers...

...which are designed to be thrown out after the first use since no one seems capable of re-packing the stuff in its original receptacle!

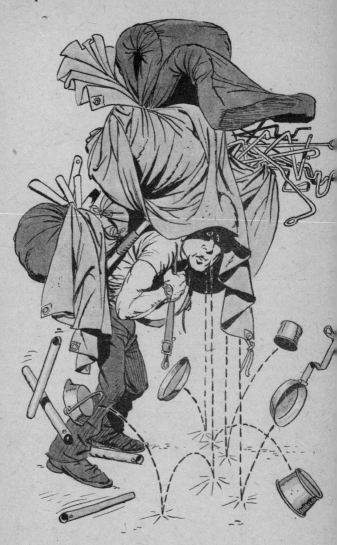

EQUIPMENT

Try to avoid duplication when equipping yourself. For instance, rather than carry several different tools, it would be wiser to invest in a Swiss Army knife which contains many of the tools you'll need...

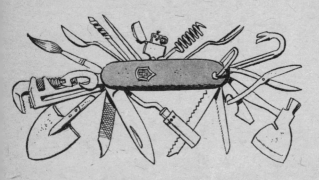

You'll also need a compass. Every book on the subject advises you to buy the best compass available! Every book but *this one!* And the reason for this is the result of extensive research. We tested over 50 compasses of the high-priced range from several manufacturers and found them *all* faulty! No matter which way we pointed them, the little needle would always spin around and point in the *same direction*—which was usually not the direction we wanted to travel in! However, we finally found a compass costing under one dollar which didn't do this—the *Kolumbus Xplorer!* No matter which way you pointed this compass, the needle didn't spin around at all, obviously making it easier to follow than the stupid spinning models!

TENTS

The kind of tent you carry is strictly a matter of personal preference. You can carry anything from a small one-man tent weighing just a couple of pounds to large tents which break down into two halves, so two members of a hiking team can each carry just half.

However if you do decide on this type of tent, be sure each member of the hiking team is carrying half of the same tent!

FLASHLIGHTS

Every hiker should have a flashlight. Strange as it seems, the person who goes on a daytime hike will need a flashlight 100 times stronger than the overnight hiker! Even a little 29¢ single-cell flashlight will show up at *night,* but you'll need *quite* a flashlight to show up in the *bright sun!*

"HIKER'S GROG"

Whether or not you carry a stove is also a matter of choice. But if you carry a stove, you also have to carry something to cook, plates to serve it on, and utensils to eat it with. To cut down on *"shlepping"* (hiker's jargon for carrying) all this stuff, make up a large thermos of *"hiker's grog"* before any trip. Anybody can make hiker's grog easily—just put the following in a blender . . .

1 box breakfast cereal
2 cans of cream of mushroom soup
2 cans of fruit salad
3 packages of iced tea
1 can of sardines
1 box prunes
6 eggs
2 onions
1 pound of liver
8 containers of yogurt
2 dill pickles
1 can orange juice

Blend for about 6 minutes and put it in a large thermos. Grog contains dozens of vitamins and you can't *believe* how many servings you get! Recently a family of four left on a one-week hiking trip with only a gallon of "hiker's grog" and, believe it or not, they came back with over *½ a gallon left!*

17

MAPS

You will have to purchase a topographic map for the area you wish to hike in. Highway maps are not good unless your idea of hiking is to walk along the 'shoulder' area of U.S. 1. As you progress on your hike you should mark down significant landmarks on your map, so you will be able to find your way back through the wilderness along your original trail...

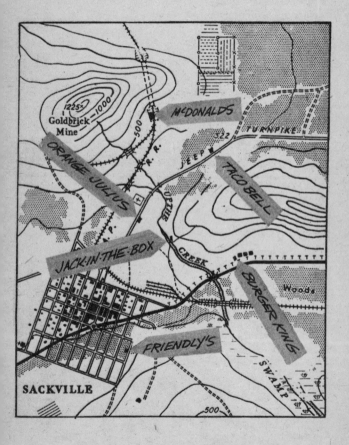

SAFETY

According to latest statistics, camping is one of the safest activities a person can engage in. Far more people are injured in the home than in the wilderness—especially when so many of the home injuries are caused by falling over the camping equipment...

Certain common sense safety rules must be observed to insure a good time for all. For instance, whenever a rope line is put up, whether to secure a tent, dining fly, or as a clothes line, it should be marked clearly so that it can be seen easily. One good way to make a line obvious is to hang equipment on it. This makes the line more visible while also providing handy storage space...

Lightning is always a hazard in the wilderness. Should an electrical storm suddenly come up, don't seek refuge under tall trees. A cave is much safer...

IN CASE YOU'RE LOST

Should you wander too far from camp and find yourself lost, don't panic. There's nothing to worry about. So you die. Big deal! Remember, there is food all around you. Watch the birds and eat what they eat—nuts, berries, fruit, worms, etc. If you're lucky, you might find a bird who has a passion for pizza.

Another useful tip is to spell out S.O.S. in large letters in a clearing so that your message can be spotted by planes. If you're not spotted soon, you might want to expand your message for help...

Remember, telephone lines and electric cables always lead you to the nearest town. By following them in either direction you'll eventually reach life—unless, of course, you find yourself in Philadelphia. In that case; you're probably better off staying lost.

SNAKES

The fear of snakes is grossly exaggerated in this country. You should note that only 4 species of the hundreds of families of snakes that exist in this region are poisonous. Of course, there are millions of those 4 species around, but chances are you'll probably get bitten by wasps, hornets, leeches, scorpions, gila monsters, or angry farmers before you'll ever get bitten by a snake, so put your fears aside and enjoy the wilderness!

CHAPTER II

SAILING

Say to the landlubber:

Tighten the jumpers and lower shrouds!

and he'll reply:

Huh?

But say to the experienced sailor:

Tighten the jumpers and lower shrouds!

and he'll reply:

Huh, SIR?!

Yes, that's just a little of the talk of the water. So you can get a feeling of *nautical jargon*, here's a sample glossary. The list is by no means complete. We just selected some terms which we felt are representative, and which we know how to spell correctly:

BOOM .. the sound you hear when your sailboat crashes into the dock.

BOW .... half of the expression used by a salty dog.

HEEL .... what a salty dog should be taught to do.

KNOT .... a nautical way to say "don't" (i.e., "do knot use this rope!")

LINE .... something to have handy when you approach the dock. You should always have good lines like "I usually don't show the master bedroom to anyone, but in your case, I'll make an exception!"

MAST . very tall pole on sailboat deck, used to get better TV reception.

SHEET . most sea stories your sailing companions tell you are just that!

POINTS OF SAILING

If a sailboat is sailing in a straight line away from the wind, this is called leeward.

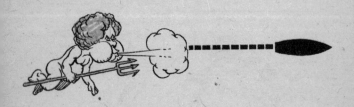

26

If a sailboard is zigzagging back and forth across the wind, this is called tacking.

If a sailboat is sailing directly into the wind, this is called miraculous.

THE FUNCTION OF FITTINGS

No two skippers agree on the choice of location of fittings, and since, depending on the size of the sailboat, there can be *hundreds* of fittings, going into detail about each would burden the new sailor's mind. The fittings you are *most* likely to come across, no matter how small the sailboat, are:

1. thing-a-ma-jig
2. thing-a-ma-bob
3. whatz-ama-call-it
4. whos-it
5. whats-it

It is worth memorizing these 5 basic terms which are not only totally interchangeable with other sailboats, but you'll find that *this kind of knowledge* serves as a basis for your understanding almost *all* other complex mechanical equipment as well!

BOTTOM DESIGN

A sailboat would tend to go sideways with the wind, so something must stop it. This is accomplished in some sailboats by a *centerboard* which can be raised or lowered at will...

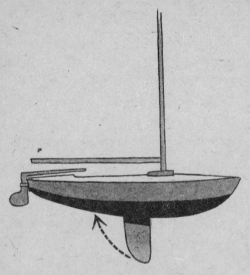

Or a sailboat may have a non-movable KEEL to furnish the required resistance to sideward sliding...

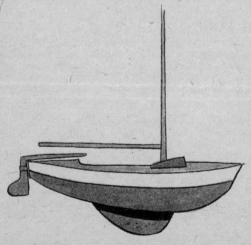

It is easy to turn a non-movable KEEL into a moving centerboard by running across submerged rocks at a good clip...

TACKING

Since it is really *impossible* for a boat to sail directly into the wind, a sailboat can arrive at a point directly upwind by making a series of *diagonal moves* one way and then the other. This is called *tacking*. The main thing to remember about tacking is that each time the boat changes "tack," the boom which holds the sail *swings wildly* across the cockpit, usually taking a member of the crew with it! That is why sailboats require large crews! When you arrive at your destination, you should have at least one crew member left to help tie up.

3. Life Preservers Overboard

1. Woman Overboard

WIND

2. Lunch Overboard

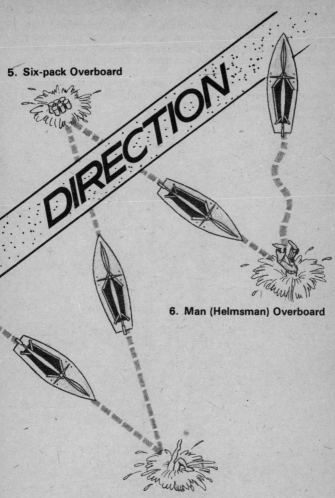

5. Six-pack Overboard

DIRECTION

6. Man (Helmsman) Overboard

4. Woman Overboard

LOSS OF WIND

If you are tacking into the wind and the boom starts across the boat for the opposite tack—but stops dead center, you will lose all forward motion and the boat will start to move *backwards*! Before you *panic*, there are some steps that can be taken:

1. Have a member of the crew circulate some *hot air* towards the sail. A good way to accomplish this is having a *politician* aboard!

2. Post a large FOR SALE sign on the boat and offer to sell it ridiculously cheap to the first boat passing by. When they tow you to shore to make the deal, tell them you changed your mind.

If both steps one and two fail, you may proceed to
3. Panic

HEELING

The more surface area of the sailboat hull that makes contact with the water, the more friction, and, consequently less speed. Study the following illustrations. You'll notice that the more the sailboat can be heeled (by having crew members shift their weight as far to one side as possible), the less hull area that comes in contact with the water. The result? Less friction and more speed!

A. MOST FRICTION

B. LESS FRICTION

C. EVEN LESS FRICTION

D. NO FRICTION

NAMES OF SAILS

A professional sailor will pride himself on knowing the correct name of each sail aboard his boat. Rather than confuse the novice with too many names at the outset, just memorize a few of the more important sails and their positions shown here.

A. Foremast
B. Fivemast
C. Sixmast
D. Pointy Part

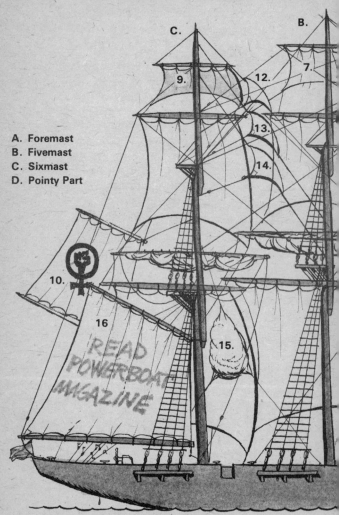

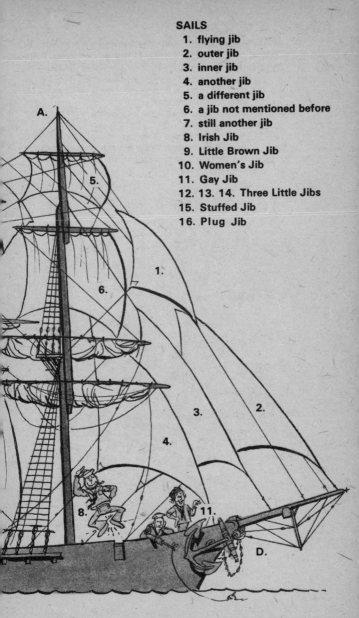

SAILS
1. flying jib
2. outer jib
3. inner jib
4. another jib
5. a different jib
6. a jib not mentioned before
7. still another jib
8. Irish Jib
9. Little Brown Jib
10. Women's Jib
11. Gay Jib
12. 13. 14. Three Little Jibs
15. Stuffed Jib
16. Plug Jib

BUYING A SAILBOAT

Sailboats have established standards of construction and are referred to as "class" boats. Class boats range from the 11½ foot PENGUIN class to 70 foot 12 Meter boats. The sailing *expert* will immediately recognize that the 70 foot boat is bigger than the 11½ foot boat, and with some practice will be able to tell that with the *naked eye*!

No matter what class boat you decide you would like to buy, here are some buying tips:

1. Knock on the hull. Does it sound *solid*? If it knocks back, avoid it! Termites make keeping a sailboat on course very difficult, especially when they're eating it while you're underway!

2. Buy from a reliable dealer. If the salesman who is going to take you for a demonstration sail in the boat you've selected shows up wearing *scuba gear*, shop elsewhere!

3. Don't buy a sailboat bigger than you and your *family can handle!*

4. On the *other hand*, don't buy a sailboat that's too *small* for your needs. Remember, once you own a sailboat, a lot of your 'long lost' friends will reappear!

5. And finally, make sure the purchase price you've agreed upon, includes *everything* you'll need to set sail!

CHAPTER III

GARDENING

Here's a leisure time activity that offers many extra benefits: you can beautify your home, apartment, or office, and, at the same time, make lasting friendships. With other people? Probably not! Other people seem to shy away from those that talk to plants! But what do you care — at least a plant can't borrow money, steal your girl, or punch you in the nose! And that makes for lasting friendships!

For those of you who still doubt what science has learned about the psychological side of plants, prove it to yourself with this simple experiment: buy two identical plants and place them side-by-side. Make sure that they both get the same amount of water, sunshine, fertilizer, etc. **But talk to one plant only!** Ignore the other plant completely for two months. Chances are the results of this treatment will be as follows...

FIRST DAY

AFTER ONE MONTH

AFTER TWO MONTHS

SELECTING A PLANT

The kind of plant you select should depend on how much light, humidity, and temperature it will receive. But no matter what plant you choose, avoid **chrysanthemums, nephrolepis,** and **spathiphyllum!** These are nice plants, but it's impossible to pronounce them correctly and you'll never spell them right when writing to others! You can't go wrong with fern.

BUYING PLANTS

There are no short cuts in the complicated procedure of buying plants. You just don't go to a nursery, drop down your cash, and walk out with the proper plants. Not if you take this kind of thing seriously, anyway. It is best you spend some time in a nursery school first.

Most plants are sold in some form of container, usually plastic or clay, and **always** drab-looking! To enhance the natural beauty of your plants it is advisable to transfer them to more creative and decorative receptacles. There are many varieties of fancy decorator pots on the market, but they are usually expensive, and worse, reflect the tastes of their creators. It is far more imaginative to create your own planters and reflect your own personality into your work. This can be done easily and without expense by utilizing objects from your home that can act as planters...

HOW TO TELL WHEN A PLANT IS SICK

There are many signs that a plant needs help. Leaf tips may turn brown... or the entire leaf may turn yellow and drop off. The plant will start to wilt, or show stunted growth. Sometimes it will break into tears at the least little thing, or pretend not to notice you. If you find that when you enter a room a plant turns its back on you, a psychiatrist is needed. You can find the name of a good psychiatrist in the telephone directory. Call him and tell him about your problems with your plant. He will either treat the plant — or you — depending upon which is in worse emotional shape!

WHERE TO PLANT

Many people who would love to have plants don't because they believe there's no place for them in their apartments. This may or may not be true. Many varieties of plants don't need direct sunlight, for instance, and can exist in places ordinarily discounted for such use...

WHAT ABOUT WINDOW BOXES?

What about them?!

TERRARIUMS

Another "garden" that requires very little room is the **terrarium.** A terrarium is a glass enclosure, whether round or square, which creates the proper balance necessary for sustaining plant life. Here too, many different types of glass enclosure can be utilized. It takes only your imagination to make it happen....

VEGETABLE GARDENING

How much space do you need to grow vegetables? "Not much," say specialists in the field. One man was able to grow several varieties on the roof of his drug store, but he had the advantage of being a farmicist. The lady pictured below is harvesting her vegetables from 8 rows of corn, 12 tomato plants, radishes, carrots, and squash. "What's so special about that?"

Here's what's so special about that....
...she accomplished this feat in a **window box!**

WHAT ABOUT WINDOW BOXES?

What about them?!

OUTDOOR GARDENING

Needless to say, outdoors offers you a larger variety of plant growth and types of gardens. Heading the list is the **formal garden.** Formal gardens are laid out in precise geometric patterns. To work in a formal garden one needs the proper tools, not to mention a tuxedo. You can't expect response from a formal garden by wearing leisure clothes. After all, it has its pride!

AFTER 3 MONTHS —
FORMAL ATTIRE

AFTER 3 MONTHS —
CASUAL DRESS

ROCK GARDENS

The rock garden is perhaps one of the most interesting types of gardens, but it is also the most difficult to cultivate. Trying to get a rock to grow is as impossible as trying to get a reader to laugh at such a bad joke, right?

AIR, FOOD, AND WATER

These are the three essentials necessary to sustain plant life. You wouldn't do so great without any of the three either, wise guy!

Air is free, but considering the quality of air today, it's still not much of a bargain!

Food is obtained from minerals in the soil, although it isn't such a bad idea to order out once in a while...

Water is provided through **nature's** own condensation/evaporation/precipitation cycle, with a little extra help from the hardware store's own faucet/hose/nozzle cycle. Indoor plants, however, especially during the winter months, suffer from lack of moisture or humidity. This can be remedied by running the shower with plenty of hot water, placing pans of water on radiators, or using a humidifier. A combination of all three will create the desired effect. For the **plant!**

PLANTING THE GARDEN

A really dedicated gardner **digs** the soil. **Really** digs it! Yeah, man! You dig?

Next, he removes all foreign matter from the proposed garden area...

Then he fertilizes the soil. This can be done by spreading commercial fertilizer (which is usually composed of chemicals) or manure. If manure is not available, copies of the Congressional Record or this book can be substituted.....

Now you're ready to plant your seeds and seedlings and watch your garden grow. In just a short time you'll reap the benefits of your efforts...

CHAPTER IV

CYCLING

The exact date of the invention of the bicycle has never been recorded, but an educated guess puts the date around the 1700 mark. An un-educated guess puts the date around 800 B.C. If nothing else, you have already learned the value of a good education! Whatever the year, that first bike looked something like this....

Of course, riding a bike of the above design was tedious work. The innovation of *rubber* tires helped considerably....

With the passing of years more refinements were made, like adding a motor...

...and two additional wheels for stability, extra space for packages, luggage, tools, etc., and a steering wheel for more control...

...not to mention a rack for carrying bikes...

TYPES OF BICYCLES

The one speed conventional bike is very heavy, and is good only for short trips on flat surfaces.

The three-speed English racer is lighter, and makes climbing hills easier than with the one speed conventional bike.

Top of the line are the very light 10 speed bikes. If you can afford the very best, one of the ultralight 15 speed bikes might be for you! And when we say ultra-light, we mean ultra-light...

A 10 or 15 speed bike makes going up hills so easy, so you'll have to find other challenges if you want to give yourself a real work out.

SELECTING THE FRAME

Bicycle frames are manufactured in men's style and ladies' style. The men's style has a straight bar across the top which makes it the strongest, by far of the two.

The ladies style has an angled top bar which was designed many, many years ago to accommodate a women wearing a long, flowing skirt. The ladies style is not nearly as strong as the men's design.

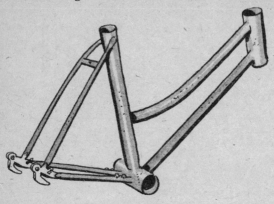

Obviously, with today's fashions the modern miss will be far better off buying the stronger man's bike.

But it *is* because of today's fashion that the ladies' style still is manufactured. It's the only thing a lot of the guys can ride!

SELECTING THE HANDLEBARS

There are two basic handlebar styles. The tourist or upright handlebar is the traditional one. Although this type of handlebar is alright for short rides, by far and away, the "drop style" handlebar is the winner for serious bicyclists.

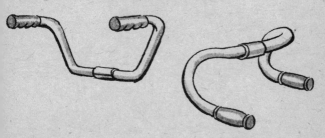

The traditional handlebar has no provision for allowing the rider to change his hand position, but more importantly the upright position of the rider creates considerable aerodynamic drag, especially with a strong headwind...

By contrast, look at the hunched-over riding position that can be achieved with the drop style handlebar. There is no aerodynamic drag here, although there is a slight problem — this man has his drop handlebars set so low that everytime he pedals, he hits himself in the face...

CYCLING AND YOUR HEALTH

This executive is rich, and consequently he moves as little as possible. Every morning his chauffer drives him to work. At only 43 years of age he is overweight, out of shape, and has just suffered a heart attack from non-use of his heart and lungs...

This man is wiser than our executive and tries to move as much as possible. Every morning he rides his bike to work, rain or shine. He does all his shopping and errands by bike. At 43 years of age he is the proper weight, in great shape, with strong heart and lungs...but unfortunately he has just been run into a tree by a chauffer trying to rush his overweight boss who just suffered a heart attack to the hospital...

GETTING IN SHAPE FOR CYCLING

Although bicycling itself will keep you in shape, there will be cold days, windy days, rainy days, etc., when you can't go out! A good way to keep in trim is with a stationary exercise cycle...

Or you can buy a rack that lifts the back wheels of your regular bike off the floor so you can pedal without moving! Just be careful, however, that the rack you buy is strong enough to hold your bike up under the strain of rugged pedaling...

ACCIDENTS WITH BICYCLES

Rather than go into lengthy details about accidents with bicycles, we suggest you experiment and find your own. Riding down the middle lane of a busy highway against the traffic is a good opener, and trying to get a large trailer truck to yield the right-of-way to you will certainly give you something to talk about with your friends, not to mention the doctors and lawyers!

ACCESSORIES

In addition to the bike, you will of course want a few accessories...

An absolute must is the addition of front and rear lights, reflectors on front, rear and sides of the bike, and on the pedals, a tire pump, a tire repair kit, a tool kit, and a tool kit carrier.

For convenience you'll need a rear metal carrier, a handlebar bag, a pair of rear saddle bags, and toe clips and straps for the pedals...

And it sure is nice to have a radio, mirror, horn, bike flag, and walkie talkie...

And finally for those times when you must leave your bicycle unattended you'll need protective devices...

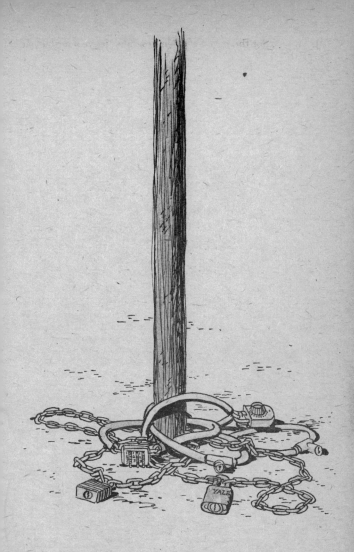

But such a well-equipped bike is sure to attract a lot of attention so even with all those protective devices, it's best to keep an eye on your bike as much as possible.

A FINAL WORD

Now you're ready to enter the wonderful world of cycling!
You've selected the right bike, the right accessories, and you're
familiar with your local rules and regulations. But it's best to
heed this final word of caution — in testing your bike and
making all the necessary adjustments, you have had to at one
time or another loosened every nut and bolt on the vehicle!
Before you set out on that big bike hike you've planned for,
make sure you tighten everything...

CHAPTER V

DRAWING & PAINTING

There's no reason that drawing and painting should be an activity for professionals only! Every professional was an amateur at one time. The key is not to be discouraged by your early efforts. Michelangelo would have been just another house painter had he been discouraged when his friends looked at his work on the ceiling of the Sistine Chapel and said, "It's nice, Mike, but it needs a second coat!"

So let us approach this subject a step at a time...

STEP ONE: Don't be discouraged with your first attempts. Use the space provided below and make a drawing...

That's your best best effort? You've got to be kidding! It's awful!

Still here? Glad to see you're not easily discouraged! That shows you have tenacity, determination, ambition, and masochistic tendencies!

STEP TWO: The reason some people find it so hard to draw things in proportion is that they have no frame of reference between the elements that make up a picture. Look at the drawing by an amateur below...

...it is easy to see the ears are too big for the head, the tail is too long for the body, the whiskers too short for the face. You might say that for an amateur it's not a bad drawing of a cat, but, as usual, you're wrong! It *is* a bad picture! This artist was trying to draw an *elephant!*

STEP THREE: There is a very easy technique to learn how to draw things in proportion. It is known as the *box technique.* Visualize drawing that same cat, but this time in a box. In this way you know approximately how much of the box should be taken up by the body, the head, the tail, etc.

See how much closer to reality the picture becomes when drawn with the box technique? It's still no elephant, but it's certainly *closer* than the previous attempt!

STEP FOUR: If you thought *proportion* was tough, wait'll you try *perspective!* Perspective is the technique that enables you to create the illusion of depth. To begin, you must first set up a *vanishing point.* One example follows:

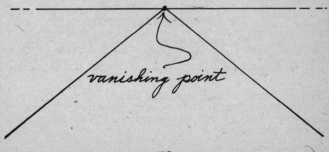

If you would like to see what a vanishing point looks like in three dimensional terms, stand at the center of a railroad track and stare at the rails until you see them "meet" in the distance. This is just an illusion, since we know the rails are parallel and never meet...

The above shows you the "vanishing point" of the last person who used this technique! His concentration was such that the illusion of the tracks meeting was nothing like the reality of the train meeting him!

Objects are drawn in perspective from the vantage point of how they're seen. Let's take an ordinary kitchen table to illustrate this point! When viewed by an average-sized adult it looks like this...

...when viewed by an average-sized child or Mickey Rooney it looks like this...

...when viewed by an average-bombed drunk it looks like this...

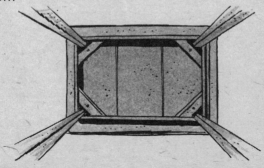

STEP FIVE: There is much that can be learned from observing the nude body. Sometimes even a little about drawing! Perhaps you have a friend or someone you work or go to school with that you can ask to pose nude for you. Explain that you are a sincere student of art, and, to show your good faith, actually attend the drawing session with a pencil and some paper. To make the "model" feel at home, you might undress also, and soft music serves to relax most people. The door should be locked to avoid distractions. All this taken care of, it's time to start *sketching!* (Well, what did you expect from a chapter entitled "Drawing and Painting!") By holding up a pencil, you can estimate proportions. For instance, from your vantage point, the model's head may be one half pencil high, the torso a full pencil, legs a pencil and a half, etc.

Now draw these relationships in your pad...

82

We can learn much about the human figure by studying the work of accomplished professionals....

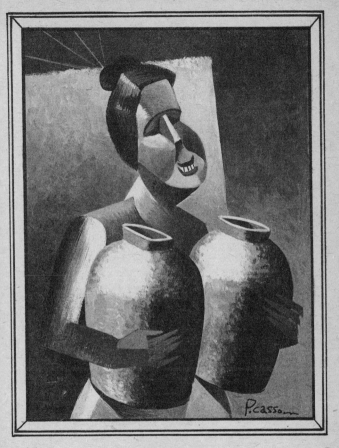

"LADY WITH LARGE JUGS"

From this picture you can learn many things; the importance of shading, backgrounds should not distract from central theme, and mainly that under the label "art" you can get away with plenty!

STEP SIX: Just as an architect must know all about the construction of a building — where the doors and windows go, beams and framework, fire exits, water lines, etc. — the artist must know about the construction of the human form. Using this principle, a drawing like the one below can be achieved...

Intelligent observation of human anatomy will help you achieve proper relationships between forms. The "average" man is about 7½ heads high, from shoulder to fingertips 2½ heads long, and his shoulders close to 2 heads wide. Using these proportions, sketch the figure.

If your drawing looks anything like the one below, perhaps you should go on to another chapter. Really, you're wasting your time!

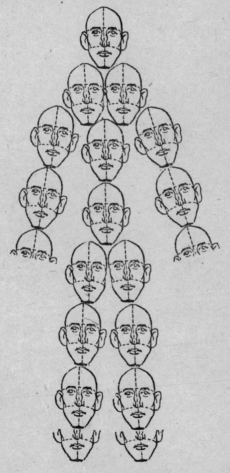

Still here? Boy, you really *did* learn about not being discouraged, discussed back in STEP ONE! See what value you're getting from this book? Wouldn't you like to buy a few extra copies for your friends?

STEP SEVEN: There are four basic shapes that exist in nature — the sphere, the cube, the cone, and the cylinder...

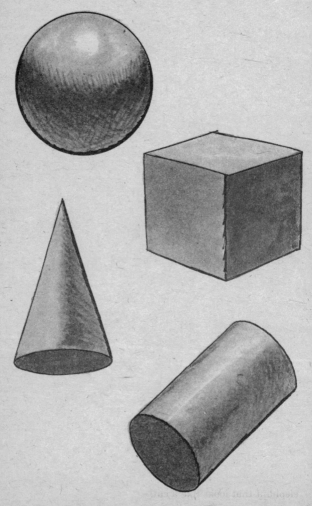

Using only these shapes, or parts from them, you can construct the human form...

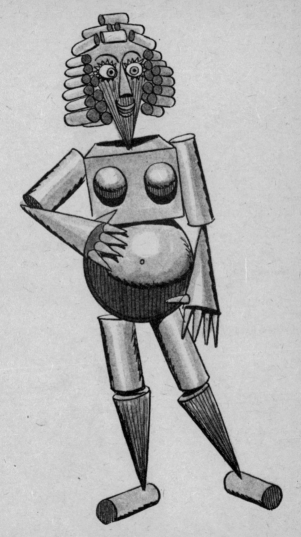

So, who said anything about "beautiful!" At least it's not an elephant that looks like a cat!

STEP EIGHT: Just like any other profession, the art field has its short cuts, techniques, and tricks to make things a little easier. For example, if a hairstyle is too difficult to draw, design a hat or head covering for the model to avoid drawing the troublesome areas...

...if the face is too difficult, draw a veil...

...if the body presents too many problems, dress her in a large shawl or a blanket...

...if the whole thing is too difficult, place the figure in a tent! There's always a way out, or better — another leisure time activity!

STEP NINE: Now that you're an accomplished sketcher, you're now ready to become an accomplished painter. Of course, you will need paints to accomplish your accomplishment. How many colors you buy needn't depend upon your budget, since a dedicated artist attempting to capture the glory of a field filled with flowers might use a hundred colors, while a less-dedicated artist painting the ocean might just use a quart of blue and a roller. Needless to say, an art critic judging both these works will unquestionably choose the painting of the ocean as "true art" for its sensitivity, reality, and emotional strength! So much for art critics!

With just a handful of colors and a little imagination* you can mix a palette of infinite range. For example...

YELLOW OCHRE BY ITSELF, STRAIGHT FROM THE TUBE

CADMIUM RED LIGHT, ALSO STRAIGHT FROM THE TUBE

MIX THEM TOGETHER, THEN ADD A TOUCH OF ULTRAMARINE BLUE...

...AND VOILA!

THIS IS WHAT PAINTING IS ALL ABOUT!

*In a black and white book, perhaps a little more imagination than usual is necessary!

STEP TEN: Well, you've mastered the art of drawing and painting, but it is important to know that so has *everyone else* who read this chapter. One way of limiting your competition is to buy out every available copy of this book to keep others from reading it! Forget about how much such an undertaking would cost! With *your talent*, you can earn it all back — maybe even more — in 20 years or so! Now, *draw your own conclusions* in the space provided below...

CHAPTER VI

GOLF

A game of GOLF consists of 18 holes and 19 arguments. In order to understand this popular leisure time activity, a knowledge of the more familiar terms is necessary.

The opening in the ground that the golf ball should end up in is called the HOLE. If you wager with those you play the game with and don't get the ball in the hole, you may wind up in the hole.

If you win, you end up in the GREEN. Trying to win by cheating on the score card is a HAZARD, and getting caught at it and being drowned in the pond is a WATER HAZARD. Or perhaps you will be shot, in which case the man with the gun makes A HOLE IN ONE, you being the one!

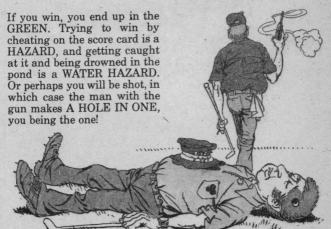

The little wooden support on which the golf ball is placed is called the TEE. A second tee is called TEE FOR TWO. Other bad puns like this will cause others around you to be TEED OFF.

Golf balls are expensive, so care must be taken not to confuse your ball with others. Most golfers write their house numbers on each one before putting them into play. This is commonly referred to as ADDRESSING THE BALL.

Jack Klix
1275 N. Elm
Dreckley Hills
N.D. 90990

Successful golfers drive to the golf course in a CADDIE. The fellow at the wheel of the CADDIE is called the DRIVER. He is usually kept in IRONS.

A wife who keeps her husband from spending all his leisure time playing is known as a GOLF BAG.

HOLDING THE GOLF CLUB

The club is gripped with the right hand (for right-handers, wrong hand for left-handers) with practically all the pressure coming from forefinger and thumb (not four fingers and thumb, stupid!). New golfers especially must learn that the club is held delicately — you should not use any more pressure than you would use holding a safety razor. The man in the following diagram is correct in that he is exerting the correct amount of pressure. His error is in trying to *shave* with the club. He must learn that certain examples shouldn't be taken literally. If we wanted him to shave, we would have suggested an electric golf club!

Once the right hand is placed correctly on the club, the left hand is then placed so that the little finger of the right hand overlaps the forefinger of the left hand. This "locking action" unifies your hands and gives you the proper grip for a smooth swing. The locking action should be released, of course, after the game or it would prove near impossible to remove your sweater.

LOCKING ACTION

LOCKING ACTION HAZARDS

THE STANCE

One way to learn the proper stance is to practice in an area that has parallel lines on the floor. In this manner, it is easier to position your feet at different angles to experience directional swinging. For instance, many golfers feel that a 20 degree angle is best for a shot straight up the middle. However, since most golf courses don't come equipped with parallel-lined greens, you'd best come up with a better method to approximate angle stances. Do you want us to supply you with *everything*?

HEAD POSITION

Diagram #1

It is obvious that the player in *diagram #1* does not have the correct golf stance. It isn't obvious to you? Well, you may be more stupid than he is — look at his head, dummy! See? He's looking *UP!* No good golfer looks up for *anything!*

Diagram #2

The man in *diagram #2* is obviously a champion golfer. Why? Because he's out cold, having just been hit with a golf ball from another player who yelled "fore." But this player took the advice from the golf greats and didn't look up for anything! Even a golf ball coming straight at his skull! Now, *that's* dedication.

THE BACKSWING

One of the most important aspects of the golf game, the backswing is learned through experience and not through even the most helpful, informative books like this one. Each golfer must discover for himself his own level of comfort and effectiveness somewhere between these two extremes:

TOO LITTLE BACKSWING

TOO MUCH BACKSWING

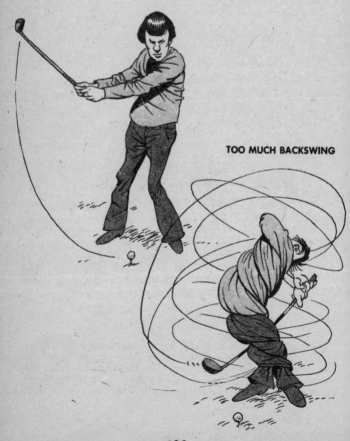

THE DOWNSWING

The same may be said of the *downswing*, the second part of this important motion:

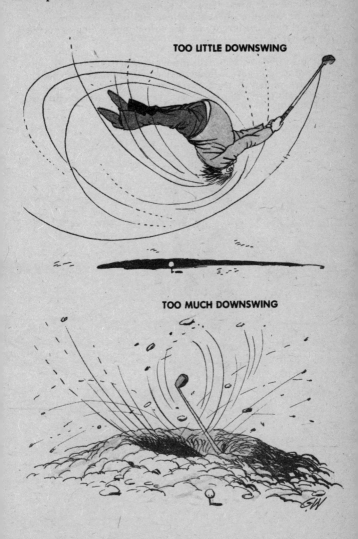

TOO LITTLE DOWNSWING

TOO MUCH DOWNSWING

THE GAME ITSELF

A game of golf consists of 18 holes. Since golf courses are usually in a "natural" area, it follows that there may be some wildlife in the area. Between rabbits, groundhogs, and the like, the course could easily have 500 holes or more, so, to make sure you're aiming for the correct hole a flag or marker is placed in it.

But don't underestimate the intelligence of our animal friends. Not wanting to get confused themselves, animals often use the markers to identify their own homes. Hitting the ball into the wrong hole can end up as a loss of a stroke. Or loss of a finger!

PAR

Every hole on a golf course falls into one of three categories: *par-three, par-four,* or *par-five.* This implies how many strokes it *should* take to make that particular hole. Since many players cannot play the course at par or under, many resort to cheating. But don't be too concerned about such practices, for in golf, lying and deception have always been par for the course.

A FINAL WORLD

Although the game of golf is very complicated, we have given you some good, basic advice. You are now ready to go on out to the golf course! If saying to yourself, "I *still* don't know" hasn't stopped all the others, why should it stop you! Besides, a 6 hour wait to play is *also* par for the course, which leaves you with plenty of time to study!

CHAPTER VII

SNORKELING

SNORKELING

Snorkeling is a relatively inexpensive way to utilize leisure time for education and adventure. With only a scuba mask, you can see the Hudson River, the Great Lakes, and the oceans of the world. Unfortunately, if you *enter* the water, you will see a lot less. But let us not begin on a *low* note. Let us, instead, pretend the waters of the world were clean, and pure, and clear, and that they weren't all polluted to the point of killing all forms of life and that soon we'll all be dead. Okay? Feeling better? Good! Now let's look at some...

EQUIPMENT

The mask

The scuba mask comes in many shapes and sizes. You should select one that fits the contours of your face, regardless of how outrageous your features may be.

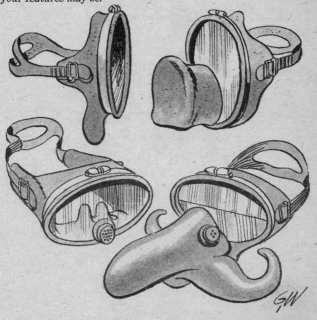

How to keep your mask from fogging

No matter what mask you use, chances are it will start to fog. The cleaner the mask, however, the less it will fog. As unlikely as it sounds, saliva cleans your mask best. You are advised to spit into it and swish the ecchy stuff around. This will keep your mask clean —unless you throw up from the disgusting practice!

What to do if your mask floods

When this happens you have two choices : 1. drowning
                                             2. clearing the mask
If you choose the first, reading the rest of this chapter will serve
little purpose. As a matter of fact, even if you chose the second
this chapter won't do much. But, for the sake of using up some of
your leisure time, let us continue. The easy way to clear a mask is
through the purge valve. This is done by simply exhaling through
your nose, forcing the air pressure to push the water out. If your
mask is not equipped with a purge valve, there are ways of clearing
your mask beneath the surface of the water. But why go into it?

**PURGE VALVE
TOO SMALL**

Fins

Fins give you added thrust for the same amount of energy exerted. Look at the diagram below. Swimmer *A* without fins kicked 100 times, but is only 35 yards from the dock. Swimmer *B* with fins kicked 100 times, but covered a distance of 115 yards.

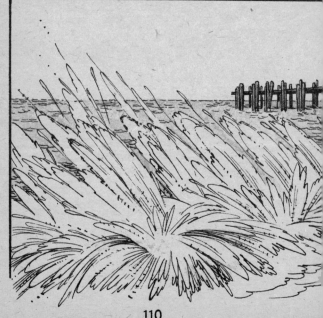

Fins come in a variety of types:
Full-foot fins   Heel-strap fins   High-heel fins   Shark fins

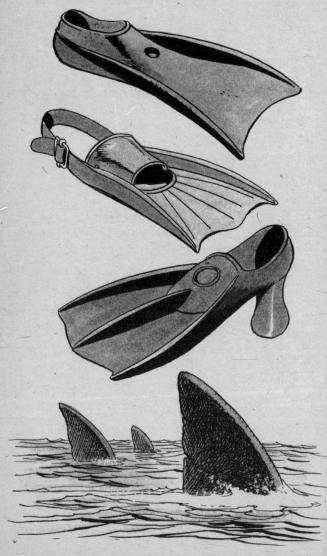

Of these four common varieties, most snorkelers avoid the third type (high-heel fins) for reasons that remain unexplained. Remember—fins that are too large will fall off too easily, while fins that are too small will *never* come off and can only be disguised by wearing very large shoes!

The snorkel

The purpose of the snorkel is to allow air from above the surface of the water to enter the lungs of the swimmer who is below the surface. By the same procedure, a fish could swim above water if he wore a snorkel that dragged below the surface. But we're not here to advise fish. Let them get their own book.

The most popular snorkel is a simple tube bent in the shape of the letter "J." If you prefer a snorkel with your own initial, like "C" or "M" you may experience some difficulties.

Clearing the snorkel

When a skin diver makes a surface dive, his snorkel tube fills with water. When the diver returns to the surface, he merely expels his breath through the tube, forcing the trapped water out through the top. He can then breathe freely. Until he gets out of the water and is confronted by those he drenched while clearing his snorkel.

The inflatable safety vest

If the skin diver becomes incapacitated for any reason, he can rely on his inflatable safety vest. *A case in point:* You have been skin diving for hours, you are exhausted, and you suddenly develop a cramp. You feel secure in the knowledge that you had bought an inflatable safety vest. You then pull the handle, the vest begins to inflate, and then comes apart at the seams. That is the moment you can kick yourself for buying the $1.49 imported model.

The point is clear—make sure you own a good inflatable safety vest before you skin dive. Below are examples of the types of quality vests used by most experts . . .

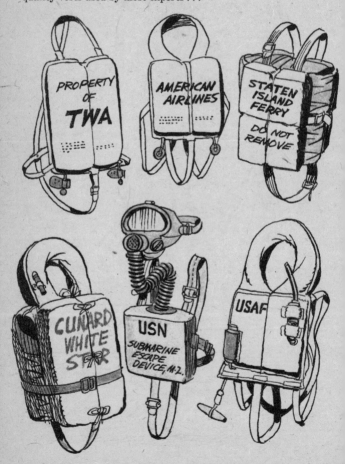

A note of caution

The inflatable safety vest contains a CO_2 cartridge that activates the vest on release. Special care must be taken in ordering replacement cartridges. *A case in point:* This diver was below the surface when fatigue overcame him. He released a CO_2 cartridge *one size too big* for his model vest. He *was* saved from drowning. Unfortunately, his ascension to the surface was too powerful and he was struck by a rescue helicopter.

Conserving air underwater

Many skin divers hyperventilate. But what they do in their private lives is no concern to us. The main way to conserve air underwater is to *relax*. Study the illustrations below. In example A, the diver is thrashing about, wasting strength, motion, and air. On a full breath he was only able to stay underwater for *15 seconds*.

The diver in example B, on the other hand, is as relaxed as it is possible to be. He is *sound asleep!* On only one deep breath he stayed underwater for *seventeen minutes*. Experts believe he may have been alive for the first *two minutes* of his dive, living proof of the advantages of relaxation underwater!

Returning to the surface

The proper way to ascend is to look up, extend one hand over your head, and turn slowly.

Notice that by extending his hand, the diver avoids coming up under a boat.

Notice also that by extending his hand, the diver has given the opportunity to the occupants of the boat to steal his expensive diver's watch.

Weight belts

Depending upon your individual buoyancy, you may need a belt that is weighted down with lead. As a safety precaution, all weight-belts come equipped with a "quick release" so that the belt falls off immediately. It is advisable that you check to see that the "quick release" pull is the proper cord.

Wet suits

Wet suits are very popular with skin divers.

Wet suits are not very popular with city-dwellers.

A "father and son" wet suit combination.

The scuba knife

When skin diving in ocean water, it is best to wear a scuba knife. The diver in illustration A is surrounded by sharks. He has no knife and can do nothing but wait in fear.

The diver in illustration B, however, *is* equipped with a knife and can therefore put it to good use. He can stab himself and get it over with in a hurry, since the knife offers no defense or protection against sharks.

Who should skin dive?

Underwater activities require a certain amount of physical skills. Before you decide to try skin diving, ask yourself these questions...

1. Can I swim 100 yards without stopping?
2. Can I retrieve a 10 pound weight from 20 feet?
3. Can I retrieve a 20 pound weight from 10 feet?
4. Can I remove a 20 pound weight from size 10 feet?
5. If I lost my mask underwater would I panic?
6. If I saw a shark would I panic?
7. How about if the shark was wearing my lost mask?
8. Do I know at least two dives?
9. Will I refrain from drinking in those two dives the night before I go diving?
10. Do I know the capital of Utah?

If you can answer "yes" to each of these questions you have what it takes to be an excellent skin diver—or at least one heck of a good liar!

Closing notes

To enjoy the pleasures of the underwater world, you will need: mask, fins, snorkel, safety inflatable vest, wet suit, weight belt, scuba knife, diver's watch, and other optional equipment. Brand new, these items can add up to quite an expensive investment. Check your local newspapers for *sales*.

There is, however, a wide variety of *used* equipment available. Check your local newspapers for *obituaries!*

CHAPTER VIII

DO-IT-YOURSELF

Look at this room filled with *beautiful furniture*! The person responsible for all of this is no different than *you* — he beleived that with a little effort, a few raw materials, and the patience to see the job through — he could have the kind of furniture he could never afford to buy ready-made from a store! Soon he was hammering, nailing, and sawing away, and at the end of *three short months* he couldn't believe his eyes — he had turned raw lumber into a vivid display of trash and debris! He then went into hock to buy the furniture you see here!

But here's the catch — he didn't have the benefit of this chapter to read before he started! If he had, well, it might have only taken him three *weeks*!

TOOLS

You probably already own a good many hand tools, perhaps even more than you think. The problem is that they've always been jumbled up in a "junk drawer" or some box on a closet shelf. The first step is to learn to treat your tools with respect and care. Sort them out, clean them up, sharpen and oil those that need it, and find a permanent place on a wall for each one, carefully labeling the area so that you'll know in an instant where each tool can be found and replaced when you're finished with it...

With a little imagination, any room can be turned into a fine home workshop!

THE WORK BENCH

Just as your tools need a place to hang, you need a place to work! A work bench is essential, but before you go out and buy an expensive, professional one, why not make use of what you have available that might easily be converted into a practical work area. This clever do-it-yourselfer has taken a rare, old French Provincial table and nailed sections of a 4' x 8' plywood sheet and some 2" x 4"s to come up with this dandy!

POWER TOOLS

"No workshop is complete without a large assortment of power tools!" The words of a home craftsman? No, the words of a major stock holder in an electric power company! But what's the difference? The truth is that it can take several minutes to cut a 4' x 8' sheet of plywood in half using a hand saw, but a power saw can do it in seconds! Just be sure you set the *depth* of cut accurately before proceeding...

NAILS

What size nail you buy will depend upon what you are nailing together. There are many different varieties of nails, each with different qualities for different purposes...

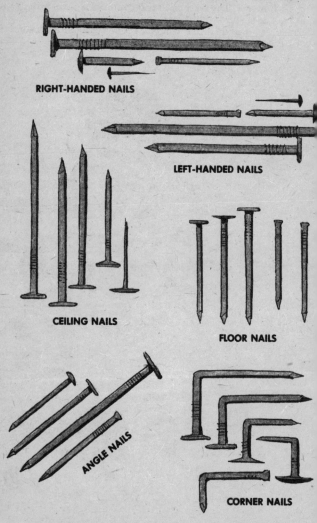

RIGHT-HANDED NAILS

LEFT-HANDED NAILS

CEILING NAILS

FLOOR NAILS

ANGLE NAILS

CORNER NAILS

SPECIAL TOOLS

The mark of a *real* home craftsman is having tools no one else has! The following are good examples of some that will make your friends and neighbors green with envy...

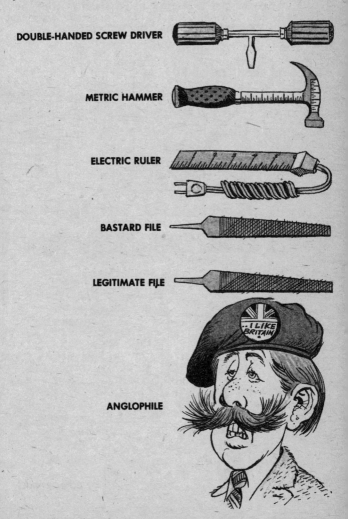

DOUBLE-HANDED SCREW DRIVER

METRIC HAMMER

ELECTRIC RULER

BASTARD FILE

LEGITIMATE FILE

ANGLOPHILE

I LIKE BRITAIN

PROJECT #1: PANELED WALLS

Here's one of the easiest jobs to tackle, and yet, the results are most dramatic. Today, just about every lumber yard stocks a large assortment of 4' x 8' panels in many shades and grains. This young couple was able to cover the walls of a 12' x 14' room in one afternoon! How long will their work hold up? Under normal conditions, years! But in this case, just as long as it takes them to take it all down, once they've become aware that they've also covered up all the doors and windows!

132

PROJECT #2: PICTURE WINDOW

To place a large, beautiful picture window in a drab, window-less wall, clearly mark off the area desired and proceed to knock out that section using a sledge hammer...

You know you've done the job correctly if you can see outside in the area you chose!

You know you've made a slight error if you can see outside *around* the area you chose!

You are now ready to fill the open area with a wooden-framed, glass window, or, if you really want to get away cheap, a few rolls of plastic wrap!

CAUTION! If you don't own the building where you wish to install the picture window, you will need permission from the landlord, or in the case of the chap below who *didn't* secure permission first, you'll need permission from the warden!

PROJECT #3: SUSPENDED CEILING

If you present ceiling is cracked beyond repair, or has gas or water pipes running across it, or a network of electric and telephone lines, you can have a brand new ceiling that will hide all these unsightly things — simply by *suspending* a new one! Using a level and a ruler, measure the *lowest point* necessary to cover it all and nail 1" x 3" strips along the sides of the wall. Then measure off other 1" x 3" pieces that will create a crosshatch of supports for the 4' x 8' sheets of plywood, tiles, or plasterboard that will serve as your new ceiling! Then nail them up! It's *that* simple!

PROJECT #4: FOUR-STORY BUILDING

Now that you've mastered the easy projects, you're ready to attempt something on a grander scale! Here's what you'll need to construct a four-story home...

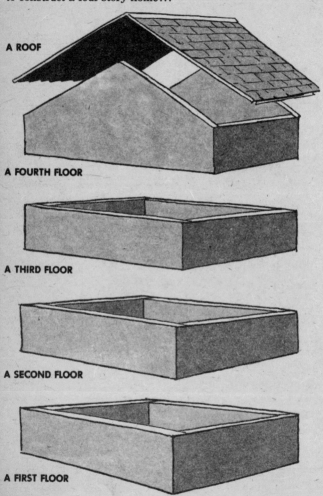

A ROOF

A FOURTH FLOOR

A THIRD FLOOR

A SECOND FLOOR

A FIRST FLOOR

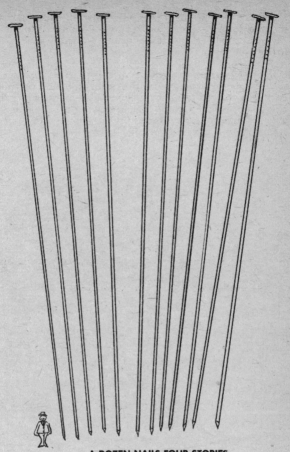

**A DOZEN NAILS FOUR-STORIES
AND SIX INCHES LONG EACH**

A LARGE HAMMER

Stack the floors in the proper order, place the roof on the top, and nail it all together making sure the nails are banged in *all the way,* since it is those last 6 inches that secure your building to the ground!

Don't be concerned that your project isn't as strong as you believe a building should be, or that it lacks some of the modern conveniences you feel should be included in every apartment today, since there's many people making a bundle on rents who are offering a lot *less* than what you've got! So put up a sign and enjoy the fruits of your labor!

CHAPTER IX

BOWLING

Experts agree— there's not too much that can be said about bowling! The ball is thrown at the pins . . .

... and the pins fall down!

We *agree* with the experts! There *isn't* too much that can be said about bowling!

CHAPTER X

WEIGHTLIFTING

There's a lot of nonsense associated with lifting weights and those who are involved in this popular leisure activity. For example, you always hear the old cliche that "a weightlifter would rather look at himself in a mirror than anything else!" You have only to go to a weightlifting workout room to see that tales like this are only 98% true!

Hi, guys, I'm from Gorgeous Unlimited and I'm taking a survey about weightlifters and their other interests! Guys? Hey, guys? Listen, the gym is on fire! Aw, c'mon fellas! Hey you with the muscles between your ears! Look — my clothes fell off! What a bunch of creeps!

Another bit of nonsense is that you must spend at least two hours a day working out or you'll lose everything! That's absurd! An hour and a half will suffice, providing you don't make a habit of cutting your sessions so short!

Another old wives tale is that if you stop working out you turn to flab. That just isn't true! This man has stopped working out for over one full week and he hasn't lost one muscle. A few of them have *shifted* a little, but *lost*, no!

What you do with your body can bring you much pleasure. What you do with someone else's body can bring you even more pleasure, but that topic won't be covered in a G-rated book!

Your reasons for lifting weights may be varied. Some do it to look better, feel better, or for self-defense. The fellow pictured below was having trouble with bullies at the beach. They would always kick sand in his face.

But just a year of weightlifting and this same fellow doesn't have trouble from bullies anymore. However, girls still kick sand in his face.

EQUIPMENT

The fundamental piece of equipment is the barbell. The barbell is simply a pipe to which the weights are attached. It is important that the barbell is equipped with a locking device to keep the weights in their proper place.

It is also very important that the bar you purchase to hold your weights is strong enough to support the weights you place on it. Don't try to limit your expenses by substituting inferior material, like broom handles.

Well-equipped gyms feature a special piece of equipment called a *universal gym* or *circuit trainer*. These machines have tracks supporting the weights permitting workouts without having to change a single barbell. It would be foolish to purchase one of these machines for your own home, since they cost so much money it would be cheaper to pay off the bullies that bother you! Then too, the equipment is difficult to master and can lead to some problems before you are able to familiarize yourself with it.

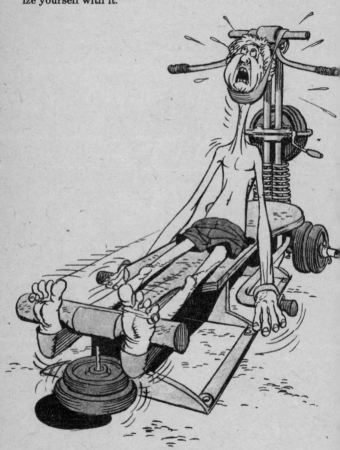

HOW MUCH SHOULD YOU LIFT?

There is no real answer to this question. How much you lift depends entirely on your individual needs. Those who want to join an expensive gym or outfit their homes with the latest, fancy equipment may have to lift more than those who are content with basic equipment, but in either case, it is best to start lifting small — like a watch or a wallet — until you can work yourself up to the bigger things!

THE SHRUG

Grab the barbell with your hands approximately shoulder-width apart. Allow the barbell to hang at arms length, then "shrug the shoulders" to the greatest height you are capable of, as if gesturing "I don't know." Repeat this exercise 10 times. Some weightlifters find it difficult to shrug their shoulders without *actual reason*. If you are one of these people suffering from similar muscle-bound intelligence, the list of questions below should offer ample shrugging opportunities:

1. Where is Billy the Kid buried?
2. What is the capitol of Warsaw?
3. How many pairs of shoes are sold each year in Utah?
4. How does a flea mate?
5. Who is John Farbotnik?
6. What was Thomas Edison's monthly electric bill?
7. Why is tonight different from all other nights?
8. When is Sandra Dee's birthday?
9. Who really cares?
10. If Cleveland was our 22nd and 24th President, when was Toledo?
11. Why can't the author count?

BENT-OVER ROWING

Standing slightly behind the barbell, bend over and grasp it with both hands approximately shoulder-width apart. Maintaining this bent-over position, pull the bar up until it touches your chest. The amount of repetitions you do is completely up to you. You will, in time, find your own level. Over-doing this exercise, however, is not recommended. The fellow below has learned this for himself . . .

BARBELL CURLS

Hold the barbell at waist level and "curl" it to the chin. This is the best exercise known for pumping up the biceps and impressing others in the shortest amount of time.

AFTER ONE MONTH

AFTER THREE MONTHS

AFTER SIX MONTHS

BENCH PRESS

Lie on your back with a bench under you keeping the barbell at chest level (see diagram). Raise and lower the barbell for as many repetitions as you desire. This exercise is known for developing both the inner and outer pectoral muscles to a very great extent, and while it might help prevent other men from kicking sand in your face at the beach, other *women* may resent you even more!

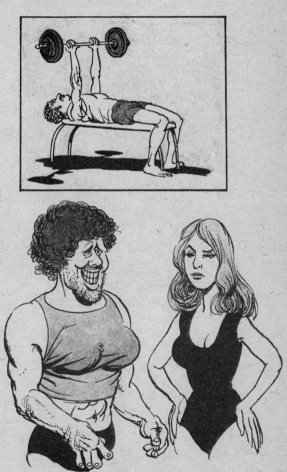

Once you get involved with weightlifting, you'll probably want more advance reading on this fascinating subject. Here are some noteworthy books worth investigating:

"Strains, Pains, and Canes" by Sid Ascher

"Weightlifting — The Only Recommended Pastime" Published by the New York Chiropractic Club

"Hernias — Single and Double" by Jacques Stroppe

"The Hunchbacks of Notre Dame" by Vic Ugo, Weightlifting Coach

"100 Good Markets for Selling Your Used Equipment" by Artie Charney

CHAPTER XI

HUNTING

What better way to prove you're a man than *hunting*!

You start out on your hunting trip with a stop at the local sporting goods store for supplies. You know the hunting season is about to begin and the prices are unreasonably high, but you pay the rip-off price and never say a word to the clerk—he's only 2″ shorter than you and you never can tell about those small, tough guys . . .

...so you stuff your guns and ammo in the car and drive up to a gas station where some nut charges you a ridiculous price for gas, but you never say a word to him — he looks a little flakey with those "love" buttons and you never can tell when one of these "peaceniks" will go off the wall and pull a gun on you...

...so you drive up to the woods, cursing at every fascist speed limit sign along the way trying to keep you from reaching your destination before the other hunters get there! At last you're there! The woods! *Now* let someone get in your way! You'll show 'em what stuff you're made of! You've been pushed around long enough! Suddenly something moves in the clearing ahead ... a squirrel! Why that little @#%/&*#@%&!!! How *dare* he roam around your turf! Your shotgun is loaded! You take aim ...

...did you get him? Does it really matter? With all that shooting, you had to have killed *something!*

Welcome to the wonderful world of *hunting!*

EQUIPMENT

You will need several types of rifles for hunting, each for a particular kind of game. For example, it would be silly to carry a big-game rifle to shoot a rabbit when a high-powered shotgun with a telescopic sight will suffice!

Get to know your guns! It takes weeks of practice for you to get the feel of each weapon, how it handles, how it sights, the trigger squeeze, the recoil, but when you do, hunting can be that much more fun. But don't wait until you're out in the woods before you learn all this! Get your practice in beforehand!

You must always remember that animals have certain advantages over hunters, so you should strive towards creating a more even balance between yourself and your game! For example, the sneaky, cunning deer uses his natural camouflage to escape detection . . .

You can counter with some man-made equipment that will turn the tide in your favor . . .

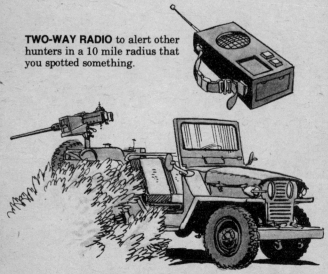

TWO-WAY RADIO to alert other hunters in a 10 mile radius that you spotted something.

JEEP or LAND ROVER to keep track of *lighting* game who can move as fast as 5 miles an hour.

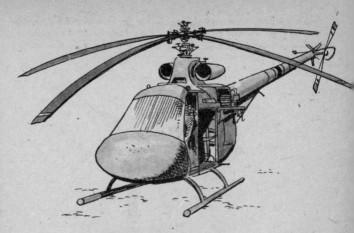

HELICOPTER to spot game from above without having to endure the terrible hazards of the brush, like poison ivy and insects.

MOBILE HOME to offer you the convenience of modern living during your strenuous trip as well as getting you close enough to the action so you can hunt from your own window.

Another way to stem the enormous tide against you is to employ *hunting dogs!* While the dogs do all the "leg work" by running down and treeing game, the hunter is still left with the tough part— pulling the trigger!

Good hunters take their equipment seriously. With so many millions of people hunting today, it would appear that animals are getting better at hiding, since so few of them are being spotted. It's almost like there are very few animals left, which, of course, could *never* be the case! In any event, sophisticated equipment is necessary to keep the balance in the hunter's favor, so spare no cost in buying the best available, even if it means cutting down on some of the other necessities, like liquor!

OTHER EXPENSES

No one said hunting was *inexpensive*! You can, as already suggested, cut expenses a bit by "roughing" it a little. One obvious way to save some cash is to take a hunting lodge further from the well-stocked game areas. True, you *may* actually have to leave your room to gun something down, but that's the breaks!

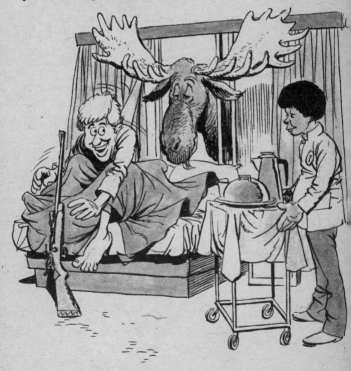

WHERE TO HUNT

Obviously, the best places to hunt are those that have the largest number of animals in the area. An ideal place is your local zoo! But be forewarned: If you do shoot some animals in your local zoo, expect a bunch of so-called "humanitarians" to raise a fuss! It is no secret that every *pleasure* on earth attracts weirdos who will always take the opposite stand! Just don't let these ecology and conservation groups get you down! Remember which group has the guns!

As silly as it may sound, you can tell if there are animals within an area by looking for fresh animal "droppings". Discovering animal droppings is very easy— It's the kind of clue that's somehow very easy to *step into*!

Here's another neat little tip! Your footsteps will tend to carry further in the direction the *wind is blowing*. To determine wind direction, take a hand full of dirt and throw it in the air . . .

The wind is blowing *away* from this hunter.

The wind is blowing *toward* this hunter.

Another great hunting area is a private ranch where, for a moderate fee, the animal of your choice is released in a fenced-in area. While this method guarantees a "take," it can also be quite *dangerous.* For instance, one hunter was seriously injured while trying to bag a wild *cow*! When the cow let out a blood-curdling "*moo*," the hunter dropped his loaded rifle and then tripped over it!

FOREST FIRES

Everyone knows who *this* is! Of course, it's *Smokey the Bear*! Smokey serves as constant reminder that all campfires should be properly extinguished before leaving the area. Some people like to blame *hunters* for many of the forest fires, but our records show that the hunter *respects* nature, and is too busy trying to *kill* than to fool around with *fires*!

STALKING

Since stalking calls into play many muscles of the body that are not normally used in day to day living, you should practice "stalking" in your living room for a week or two before the hunting season opens. You can learn the best stalking techniques by crawling under sofas, chairs, night tables and other low furniture in your home . . .

However, practice is only practice! Becoming too adept at a skill in one's *living room* can be limiting, unless, of course, you create a *similar environment* in the woods . . .

DRIVING

There is a hunting method to "*collect*" all the animals within a given area and this is called "*driving*"! A group of hunters is divided into two teams: one team stands guard at a clearing, a road, or a border line! The other team forms a line and stalks the animals within the area, driving them toward the first group. When the animals are in sight of both groups, all *open fire*!

This method, of course, relies on a good deal of skill for *both* teams!

SHOOTING FROM A BLIND

If you do not want to roam the woods looking for prey because you fear you might be attacked by *the king of beasts—your fellow hunter*, you can shoot from a blind! A blind is a hiding place for the hunter, camouflaged to look like the surrounding background. A really swell blind is shown here . . .

That's right, that clump of bushes is really a hide-out for hunters. It certainly fooled the animals. Unfortunately it also fooled a group of passing hunters who heard a noise coming from within and opened fire on it . . .

THE KILL

Oh, boy, we're finally here! The *neat part*! The *kill*! Once you have the animal in your sight, squeeze the trigger *firmly*, but don't get excited and *jerk it*! Try to hit the animal in a vital spot, otherwise you may just injure him and he'll go tramping through the woods limping and bleeding, and just how far does *he* think *you* feel like walking to finish him off!

AFTER THE KILL

Immediately upon bringing down an animal, slit it's throat and hang it upsidedown! This will make it bleed quickly and well to prevent *spoiling*! The hunters below have followed this important rule. One of the hunters is deciding where to go to find *another* deer to slay! The others are seriously considering becoming *vegetarians*!

A FINAL WORD

There seems to be a growing feeling in this country that hunting isn't really a *sport*. This feeling is, of course, *nonsense*! So the animal can't defend itself— *big deal*! So an animal can't equip itself — *big deal!* Just remember, animals are *dumb!* They're just plain stupid! And anything stupid doesn't *deserve* to live!

CHAPTER XII

FLYING

Your airplane streaks down the runway! You pull back on the wheel and suddenly you're airborne! It's your first solo flight — you control your own destiny! You check out the gauges, remembering the first impression you had when you saw the complex board and thought you'd never be able to master it! But now you're on your own, but not really, for you and your plane have become *one*...

...and seconds later you and your plane and the control tower have become *one* as you crash into it! But it was a good lesson you have just learned — never get so involved with the *romance of flying* that you don't look where you're going!

How do commercial pilots ignore the *romance of flying?* Only with great difficulty, considering the pretty stewardesses in their sexy uniforms always hanging around in the cockpit! But that's *their* problem! Worry about you *own* problems, like getting someone to rent or lend you a plane after what you just did to the one on your first solo flight!

WHY LEARN TO FLY?

You have only to look down at the bumper-to-bumper traffic on the roads below to answer *that* question. A 3 hour drive from one city to another will take you under an hour to travel the same distance!

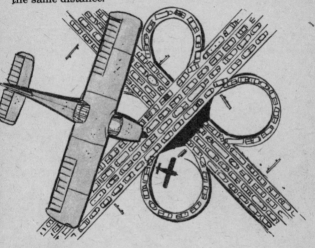

True, you may have bumper-to-bumper traffic in the *air,* too, and wait 3 hours in a circling pattern before given permission to land, but you *can't* compare the pleasure of "stack-up" to the boredom of car traffic!

True, once you *do* land, you have to use *those same roads* the car traffic is stalled on in order to reach your destination, but you can't compare the pleasure of car traffic to the boredom of "stack-up!"

Another advantage of flying is that you won't have to settle for the common, dull vacation spots everyone else goes to! You'll be able to go off the beaten path to new, unexplored vistas...

For the businessman, the private plane is *ideal!* Instead of making an impersonal phone call, imagine the impact you make on your client when you fly to his city for a personal meeting...

And for the "free of spirit," flying can't be beat! He is an individual, independent — there's no one to tell him where and when to go...

THE LANGUAGE OF FLYING

When you first go to a private airport and hear the pilots talking, you will be introduced to a whole, new *language!* Words like quadrant, radial, omnidirectional, paella, and muchacho will sound foreign to you, but, before you know it, you will soon be using those same words! Of, course, you *still* won't know what they mean, but at least you can enjoy making the *novices* feel as stupid as you once did!

WHY DOES AN AIRPLANE FLY?

Air exerts pressure on everything around it approximately one ton per square foot. And there are other forces at work, too. Study the following diagrams...

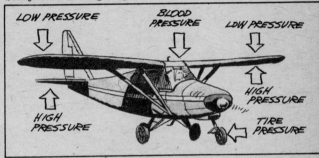

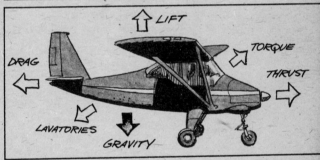

Now you know why a plane flies! But so much for the *simple* stuff! From here on in, things get to be a little more *difficult*!

WHAT ABOUT WINDOW BOXES?
See page 54

When an automobile driver gets into his car, he rarely checks anything! He doesn't have to as long as he has gas in the tank. He merely turns the ignition key and away he goes. Not so with flying! There's no way you can do that with a plane! A sample safety check list follows:

1. Is everything neat in the glove compartment?
2. Are the ashtrays empty?
3. Is the radio tuned in to my favorite "rock" station?
4. Do I have enough snacks, candy, gum, etc.?
5. Am I inside the airplane?

If you're answer to at least 3 of the 5 questions is "yes," you're ready to fly! CAUTION: Your personal safety if not your *life* depends upon serious analysis of your checklist! Don't — REPEAT — don't fool yourself by taking off with less than 3 out of the 5 questions unequivocally marked "yes!"

INSTRUMENTS

No matter how small the aircraft, the novice will find the instrument panel a bewilderment of dials and gauges. A sample instrument panel from a small plane follows...

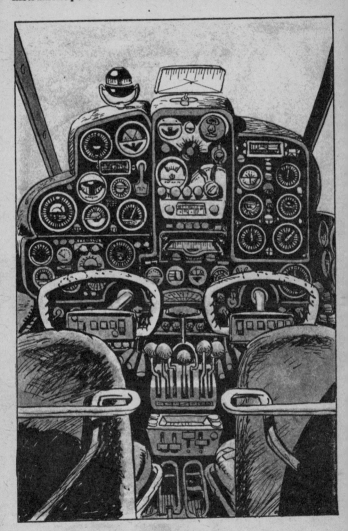

You're probably thinking, "If that's the instrument panel of a *small* plane, what does an instrument panel on a *large,* commercial jetliner look like?" If you're not thinking that, then you're not being *cooperative* and your *nose should bleed!* A typical panel of a jumbo jet follows...

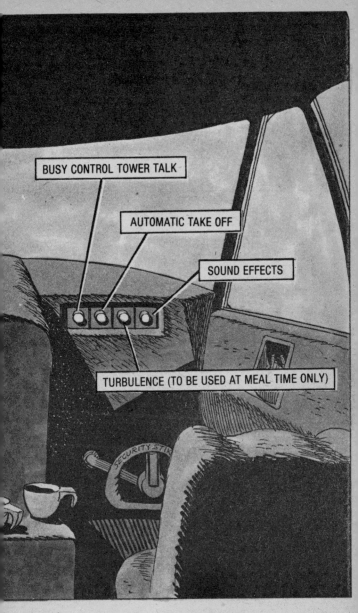

183

CONTROLS

You must learn *controls!* You must not *panic!* You must *obey orders!* You must not *cry!* You must *clean your room!* Some other controls that might prove useful to you during your first solo flight are:

THE TRIM CONTROL There is a crank that controls the plane's *trim.* It is used for raising or lowering the *nose* of the plane to maintain level flight. The plane below is in perfect trim...

Some of you more sharp-eyed readers may have noticed that the top of the picture contains some *odd shapes.* Closer examination will reveal those shapes to be the tops of *buildings.* That would indicate that the plane is in perfect trim, only *upside down.* This condition makes eating snacks or landing more *difficult!*

THE WHEEL The wheel in a plane looks and functions like the wheel in a *car* — turn it *right*, the plane turns *right*; turn it *left*, the plane turns *left!* But here's the difference — pull back on the wheel and the plane goes *up!* If you can do that with your car also, we suggest you fly it back to Detroit for a full check-up!

THE PARKING BRAKE Again, just like in an automobile, the plane has a parking brake which secures the vehicle after a full stop has been achieved. The novice must realize that this procedure must only be used on the *ground!*

THE LOG BOOK

It is a regulation that all pilots maintain a log book, entering records of training, hours of instruction received, flight time, etc. Each and every occurrence is entered from the time you reach the airfield to the time you leave. A sample follows...

LOG BOOK OF: *ALLAN JAFFEE*

DATE: *7/30* TIME: From *1315 HRS* to *1349 HRS*

AIRCRAFT # *N 567572·F*

COMMENTS: *TOOK OFF LOW. AMONG THE THINGS I TOOK OFF WAS THE TOP OF THE LOCAL CHURCH, THE TOP OF THE POST OFFICE AND THE WEATHER VANE ON BOB BECKER'S BARN*

LOG BOOK OF: *ALLAN JAFFEE*

DATE: *8/15/72* TIME: From *0900 HRS* to *0920 HRS*

AIRCRAFT # *N 20693-G*

COMMENTS: *I'VE REALLY GOT THE HANG OF TAKING OFF HIGH. MAYBE A LITTLE TOO HIGH --- FLEW RIGHT INTO THE CARGO HOLD OF A 747 --- ENDED UP IN ROUMANIA -- WITH NO PASSPORT.*

LOG BOOK OF: *ALLAN JAFFEE*

DATE: *12/13* TIME: From *1430 HRS* to *1434 HRS*

AIRCRAFT # *N 609773-P*

COMMENTS: *WELL, TODAY I MADE THE BEST TAKE-OFF OF MY LIFE! NOT TOO LOW, NOT TOO HIGH --- IF ONLY I HADN'T BEEN IN THE HANGAR WHEN I DID IT!! FLYING SCHOOL HAS ASKED ME NOT TO BOTHER*

THE TAKE-OFF

You've checked and double-checked *everything!* Your instructor hands you the microphone! You switch it on and say...

If the men in the control tower break up, they'll give you permission to take off. They are a fun group who enjoy a good laugh! However, you can also expect similar treatment when you're in *serious trouble* and you call down for instructions...

The take-off is one of the more challenging parts of flying, since there is a lot going on. The flight itself is more often than not a *bore*. That is why commercial airlines show movies, pass out newspapers and magazines, serve meals, etc. It would be wise for you to do the same...

THE LANDING

Most airfields are bounded by buildings, trees, power lines, etc., so you'd best overcome your fear of skimming over high objects than to make the vertical approach pictured below...

Landing is also the time most people *panic*. Screaming, sweating, throwing up, and fainting is *common!* The *real* problems start when it is the *instructor* doing the screaming, sweating, throwing up and fainting!

SUMMARY

You now have a good idea of what it's like to fly. Despite the confusion, hardships, fear, and all the rest, there you are at the airfield the following week, ready to fly *again!* Only *this* time you've bought a ticket and left the piloting to others *less capable* than yourself! You're finally *wising up!*